FOOD BRANDS WE LOVE

OREO

By Kaitlyn Duling

Kaleidoscope
Minneapolis, MN

The Quest for Discovery Never Ends

This edition is co-published by agreement between Kaleidoscope and World Book, Inc.

Kaleidoscope Publishing, Inc.
6012 Blue Circle Drive
Minnetonka, MN 55343 U.S.A.

World Book, Inc.
180 North LaSalle St., Suite 900
Chicago IL 60601 U.S.A.

Kaleidoscope ISBNs
978-1-64519-216-9 (library bound)
978-1-64519-284-8 (ebook)

World Book ISBN
978-0-7166-4194-0 (library bound)

Library of Congress Control Number
2020936219

Developed and produced by Focus Strategic Communications Inc.

Printed in the United States of America.

Bigfoot lurks within one of the images in this book. It's up to you to find him!

TABLE OF

CONTENTS

Chapter 1
One Tough Cookie

Cameron poured a tall, cold glass of milk. He grabbed a plate from the cabinet. Then he went to the pantry. It was time to eat some Oreos.

Frowning, Cam scanned the rows of food. Pasta, onions, beans, rice, crackers, cereal. In the corner, he spotted a candy bar made with Oreos. There was a pan of brownies made with Oreo pieces. Those were delicious, but they weren't what Cam wanted. Opening the freezer, he saw Oreo-flavored ice cream. There was even a box of Oreo Ice Cream Sandwiches. But he couldn't find any Oreo cookies.

You can't have Oreos without a glass of milk.

Oreo cookies are sold in countries around the world, including China.

Cam slumped at the kitchen table. Oreo was one of the biggest **brands** on Earth. In fact, Cam had recently read that Oreo was the #1 best-selling cookie brand in the world. His parents and grandparents loved them. His little sister ate them. Why couldn't he find any in the house?

Last year, in sixth grade, Cam's teacher had talked about Oreo's **international** success.

FUN FACT

40 billion Oreo cookies are produced each year. That's enough to circle the earth five times.

He brought in some green tea ice cream Oreos from China. Another student brought banana-flavored Oreos from Argentina. Both were good, but Cam still liked the original. His mouth watered. He thought of the sweet cream filling and the crisp, chocolate discs. The glass of milk sat on the counter. Where could they be?

Oreos and milk are a bedtime snack for a lot of people.

There is a reason Oreo claims to be "milk's favorite cookie." Most of us can't imagine one without the other.

Suddenly, Cam had an idea. Snapping his fingers, he ran to the living room. It wasn't by the door. It wasn't next to the couch. There. On the stairs, Cam spotted his dad's briefcase. Popping it open, he found the lost treasure. A half-empty package of Oreos. Sometimes Cam's dad took Oreos to work for an afternoon snack. Cam shook his head and laughed. Like father, like son. Now where was that glass of milk?

FUN FACT

It takes exactly 59 minutes to make one Oreo. Oreos are made at plants in Virginia, Oregon, New Jersey, Canada, and Mexico.

Chapter 2

History of Oreo

Oreo cookies are an American **icon**. But their story is just over 100 years old. The Oreo story starts back in 1898. At that time, cookies and crackers were becoming popular in the US. Several baking companies decided to **merge**. At the time, crispy crackers and cookies were often called "biscuits." So the new company was named the National Biscuit Company, or Na.Bis.Co. What does that sound like? Nabisco. It was located in New York City. Nabisco became famous for Barnum's Animal Crackers.

Barnum's Animals Crackers were first introduced in 1902, named for the Barnum and Bailey Circus.

This National Biscuit Company advertisement first appeared in 1901.

WHAT'S IN A NAME?

Where did the name "Oreo" come from? There is no firm answer. Some think it came from "or." That's the French word for "gold." The early packages were gold. Others think the name combines the "re" from "cream" and the two "o"'s in "chocolate. A third theory says that the Greek word for "hill" is "oreo." Oreos were originally shaped like a baseball mound.

About 10 years after the success of their animal crackers, Nabisco had a new idea. Well… it wasn't exactly new. There was already a cookie that looked and tasted a lot like Oreos. It was called Hydrox. Hydrox was created in 1908 by the Sunshine Biscuits Company. Sunshine was Nabisco's **competitor**.

In 1912, Nabisco released their "new" recipe: the Oreo Biscuit. It was very similar to the Hydrox.

Hydrox cookies were similar to Oreos, but less successful.

It had white cream filling. It had two chocolate discs. The Oreo Biscuit was sold in a yellow tin with a glass cover. Nabisco has always denied that the Oreo idea was stolen from Hydrox. But the history says otherwise.

Unlike Hydrox, Nabisco's new cookie was a hit. Its popularity grew. Soon, sales of the Oreo outpaced Hydrox. Today, Oreo is the world's most popular cookie.

FUN FACT

Oreo's 100th birthday was in 2012. To celebrate, Oreo released a birthday cake flavor. The cookie featured—what else—sprinkles.

OREO BRAND TIMELINE

1908
Hydrox cookies are first sold by the Sunshine Biscuits Company.

1912
The first Oreo cookies are sold to a grocer in Hoboken, New Jersey.

1921
The Oreo Biscuit is renamed. It becomes the Oreo Sandwich.

1923
Oreo ads on trolley cars are the first to feature “the twist.”

1948
The cookie’s name changes again, to the Oreo Creme Sandwich.

1975
The Double Stuf Oreo is introduced.

1976
Stores begin to sell football-shaped Oreos.

1980
A new slogan appears: “For the Kid in All of Us.”

1908 1912 1921 1923 1948 1975 1976 1980

1987 1991 1995 1997 2004 2008 2012 2019

1987
Fudge-covered Oreos appear on shelves.

1991
The bite-sized Oreo Mini is first sold.

1995
Oreo does a major package redesign. The 1995 package is the one in use today.

1997
Oreo removes pork fat from the cream recipe.

2004
The slogan "Milk's Favorite Cookie" is introduced.

2008
The Oreo Facebook page is created.

2008
Oreo produces its first Super Bowl commercial.

2012
Oreo celebrates its 100th birthday with special commercials and flavors.

2019
Oreo introduces the Most Stuf Oreo, filled with four times the amount of cream filling.

Chapter 3

Twist, Dunk, Eat

Annie's eyes widened. It was snack time at her after-school program. Snack was her favorite part of the day. What could make it even better? The snack of the day was Oreos. Carrots and dip were tasty. Annie liked crackers and cheese. But Oreos and milk were the ultimate snack.

Annie picked up her first Oreo. She carefully twisted the two sides. "Pop." The cookie opened without breaking. Perfect. Looking up, she started to lick the cream off of the cookie. But her mouth dropped open. Across the table, her friend Talia was **dunking** her entire Oreo in milk.

It is hard to resist dunking your Oreo in milk.

There are many ways to eat Oreos.

Looking down the table, Annie was shocked. She watched Jason break the cookie down its middle. Colin popped the whole cookie in his mouth. Shay managed to dunk her cookie and then break it open. Everyone had a different style. Jerry was the wildest of all. He put all three of his Oreos into a stack. Then he put the whole stack in his mouth. Gross.

FUN FACT

According to Kraft, 50 percent of Oreo eaters pull apart their cookies before they eat them.

Oreo Peanut Butter Creme cookies are a tribute to the 1998 film, The Parent Trap. *In this movie, twin sisters Hallie and Annie eat their Oreos with peanut butter.*

After she licked off the cream, Annie ate the chocolate wafers. She ate each Oreo the same way. She tried to remember her first Oreo. Had she always twisted them open? Why didn't she dunk them in milk? Was there a wrong way to eat them?

Snack was almost over. Annie cleaned up her crumbs. Something caught her eye in the corner. It was Ms. Green, the after-school teacher. She was eating her Oreos…with peanut butter. Annie shook her head. There must be countless ways to enjoy an Oreo.

PORK FAT

Can you believe it? The original Oreo cream filling recipe included pork fat. Anyone who did not eat meat was out of luck. Those who kept kosher couldn't eat Oreos. In the mid-1990s, the company switched to a new recipe. Today, the cookies contain no animal products.

Chapter 4

Living in an Oreo World

Elle loved to go to the grocery store. Sometimes Dad let her choose a treat. “Elle,” Dad said, “Why don’t you pick out some cookies?” Elle grinned and walked as fast as she could. Her shoes

squeaked on the shiny floor and she rounded the corner. Her heart beat fast. Finally. There it was: the cookie aisle.

FUN FACT

In 2002, a portion of Ninth Avenue in New York City was renamed "Oreo Way." It marks the original site of Nabisco headquarters. The area is now part of the famous Chelsea Market.

There have been many different flavors of Oreos over the years. One source lists more than 85 flavors!

Lemon Creme Oreo was first introduced in 1920, but was discontinued in 1924; it was reissued for a limited time in 2012.

Tilting her neck back, Elle took in the massive wall of cookies. There were dozens of brands. She spotted Oreos, her favorite. They came in tons of **varieties**. There were Oreos stuffed with extra cream filling and thin Oreos that were crispy. Some were made with chocolate discs, while others had vanilla discs. The "Heads or Tails" Oreos had both.

Elle's eyes swept the flavors. Root Beer Float? Fruit Punch? Apple Pie? One package had a picture of a jelly donut on it. Another was supposed to taste like waffles. Elle wasn't too sure about all the flavors. But it did make her job more fun. She thought hard about the Oreo-flavored brownies and ice cream cones and candy bars. Dad had said "cookies." Hmm.

FUN FACT
Oreos are sold in more than 100 countries.

Oreo flavors include Mint Creme and Red Velvet. Red Velvet was released for Valentine's Day in 2015.

After at least 10 minutes, Elle finally had her choice. She grabbed the package off the shelf and returned to her dad. "Perfect choice." He placed the package of original Oreo cookies in the cart. "You can never go wrong with the classic Oreo."

ALMOST #1 (IN THE US)

Oreos are popular. In fact, in 2017, Oreo sales were the second-highest among cookie brands in the US. Which cookie beat out the mighty Oreo? "Private label" brands, or generic cookies. Chips Ahoy was #3, while BelVita and Oreo Double Stuf rounded out the top five.

OREO COOKIE PIE RECIPE

FOR THE CRUST:

You can also buy a pre-made oreo cookie crust from the store.

- 25 Oreo cookies (the wafers and fillings)
- 5 tbsp unsalted butter (melted)

FOR THE FILLING:

- 8 oz cream cheese
- 3/4 cup powdered sugar
- 2 cups whipped topping
- 10 Oreo cookies (chopped)

DIRECTIONS:

1. Place the Oreo cookies in a large Ziploc bag and crush them with a rolling pin.

2. Mix the crushed Oreo cookies with the melted butter. Press the mixture into the bottom and up the sides of a 9-inch pie plate. You can use the bottom of a glass cup for this.

3. Place the crust in the fridge while you make the filling.

4. In a large bowl, beat together the cream cheese and powdered sugar until soft. With a spoon, mix in the whipped topping, followed by the chopped Oreo cookies. You can leave some of the Oreo pieces bigger, but also include the tiny crumbs!

5. Remove the pie crust from the fridge and spoon the filling into the pie crust. Smooth the top. Place the entire pie in the fridge to chill for at least an hour before serving.

BEYOND THE BOOK

After reading the book, it's time to think about what you learned. Try the following exercises to jumpstart your ideas.

THINK

THAT'S NEWS TO ME. New Oreo flavors are introduced every year. Consider how you learn about new foods and brands. What information can be found in news articles? What about news programs on TV? Where can you go to find news you can trust?

CREATE

PRIMARY SOURCES. Primary sources provide firsthand accounts of an event. Interviews, videos, and photographs are all examples of primary sources. Create a list of the kinds of primary sources you might be able to find about Oreo.

SHARE

WHAT'S YOUR OPINION? The text states that there are countless ways to enjoy an Oreo. Do you agree with that statement? Provide evidence from the text to support your opinion. Share your position and evidence with a friend. Does your friend find the argument convincing?

GROW

DRAWING CONNECTIONS. Create a diagram that shows and explains connections between Oreo and Hydrox. How does learning about the history help you better understand Oreo?

RESEARCH NINJA

Visit www.ninjaresearcher.com/2169 to learn how to take your research skills and book report writing to the next level.

RESEARCH

DIGITAL LITERACY TOOLS

SEARCH LIKE A PRO
Learn how to use search engines to find useful websites.

FACT OR FAKE?
Discover how you can tell a trusted website from an untrustworthy resource.

TEXT DETECTIVE
Explore how to zero in on the information you need most.

SHOW YOUR WORK
Research responsibly—learn how to cite sources.

WRITE

GET TO THE POINT
Learn how to express your main ideas.

PLAN OF ATTACK
Learn prewriting exercises and create an outline.

DOWNLOADABLE REPORT FORMS

Further Resources

BOOKS

Bullis, Amber. *Mindfulness and Food*. Minneapolis, MN: Jump!, 2020.

Carole, Bonnie. *Junk Food, Yes or No*. Vero Beach, FL: Rourke Educational Media, 2016.

Kenney, Karen Latchana. *Food Scientist*. Minneapolis, MN: Jump!, 2019.

Mattern, Joanne. *Chocolate Chip Cookies*. Hopkins, MN: Bellwether Media, 2020.

WEBSITES

FACTSURFER

Factsurfer.com gives you a safe, fun way to find more information.

1. Go to www.factsurfer.com.
2. Enter "Oreo" into the search box and click
3. Select your book cover to see a list of related websites.

Glossary

brand: The name of a product made by a company.

competitor: A company that sells similar products or services.

dunking: Dipping something into a drink, soup, or other liquid.

generic: A product that has no brand name.

icon: An important image or symbol that represents something.

international: Relating to two or more nations or to countries around the world.

kosher: Jewish law regarding food that is acceptable to be consumed by a Jew, including contents, preparation, and service.

merge: Combine or unite things together, as when two companies become one.

varieties: Different kinds of things, such as the types of flavors.

Index

PHOTO CREDITS

The images in this book are reproduced through the courtesy of: lenscap67/iStockphoto, front cover (Mini Oreo), p. 31; jfmdesign/iStockphoto, front cover (packaged Oreos, Golden Oreo); Din Mohr Yaman/Shutterstock Images, front cover (Oreo ice cream cone); inkanya Anankitrojana/Shutterstock Images, front cover (Oreo cookies), p. 1; foxaon1987/Shutterstock Images, p. 1 (background); MATHATHIR MOHD YASIN/Shutterstock Images, pp. 3, 7 (top); PeopleImages/iStockphoto, pp. 4-5; Denis Michaliov/Alamy Stock Photo, p. 4; Nicholas Maderna/Shutterstock Images, p. 6; rlat/Shutterstock Images, p. 7 (bottom); Keith Homan/Shutterstock Images, pp. 8-9, 14 (bottom right), 15 (top right), 20 (top), 26 (S'mores Oreo); Albo/Shutterstock Images, p. 9 (top); Ryan Remiorz/CP/AP Images, p. 9 (bottom); David Tonelson/Shutterstock Images, p. 10; Bettmann/Getty Images, p. 11; Spacefem/CC BY-SA 3.0, pp. 12, 14 (top left); Zety Akhzar/Shutterstock Images, p. 13; dean bertoncelj/Shutterstock Images, p. 14 (top right); Artissara/Shutterstock Images, pp. 26, 14 (bottom left); Yellow Cat/Shutterstock Images, p. 15 (bottom left); Jim.henderson/Public domain, p. 15 (bottom right); ssj414/iStockphoto, p. 16; AHPhotosWPG/Shutterstock Images, p. 17; Ilina Yuliia/Shutterstock Images, pp. 18-19; artiss/iStockphoto, p. 19; rafastockbr/Shutterstock Images, p. 20 (Oreo cookies); MaraZe/Shutterstock Images, p. 20 (peanut butter jar with knife); Krasowit/Shutterstock Images, p. 21; Zety Akhzar/Shutterstock Images, pp. 22-23, 24; Michael Gordon/Shutterstock Images, p. 23; BWM Infinity/Shutterstock Images, p. 25; DenisMArt/Shutterstock Images, p. 26 (top background); LunaseeStudios/Shutterstock Images, pp. 14, 26 (Fudge Covered Oreo); P-fotography/Shutterstock Images, p. 27.

About the Author

Kaitlyn Duling twists and dunks her Oreos. She has written over 100 books for children. She lives in Washington, DC.